Double Life

Double Life

poems

DANIEL TOBIN

LOUISIANA STATE UNIVERSITY PRESS
BATON ROUGE
2004

Manufactured in the United States of America
First printing

DESIGNER: Barbara Neely Bourgoyne
TYPEFACE: Sabon
PRINTER AND BINDER: Thomson-Shore, Inc.

Library of Congress Cataloging-in-Publication Data:
Tobin, Daniel.
Double life : poems / Daniel Tobin.
p. cm.
ISBN 0-8071-2955-0 (cloth : alk. paper) — ISBN 0-8071-2956-9 (pbk. : alk. paper)
I. Title.
PS3570.0289D68 2004
811'.54—dc22

2003015404

The paper in this book meets the guidelines for permanence and durability of the Committee on Production Guidelines for Book Longevity of the Council on Library Resources. ♾

My thanks to the editors of the following journals and anthologies in which poems from this volume have previously appeared, occasionally in different versions or under different titles: *Bellingham Review:* "Myth of the Flood"; *Birmingham Poetry Review:* "Articles of Faith"; *Black Warrior Review:* "The Locksmith," "Near Forty"; *Borderlands:* "Brief Elegy for a Subdivision"; *Cimarron:* "Rooms"; *Columbia:* "At the Egyptian Exhibit"; *Crab Orchard Review:* "New World," "First Conversion," "Utopias," "Second Conversion," "Last Rites"; *The Cresset:* "Days of Creation," "House Hunting"; *Cumberland Poetry Review:* "Five Exegetical Poems," "Miranda," "The Visit"; *DoubleTake:* "Keats's Coffee Shoppe"; *Green Mountains Review:* "A Baptism"; *Image:* "Homage to Bosch"; *Laurel Review:* "Pigeons"; *Marlboro Review:* "Deep Shit"; *The Nation:* "The Hunt Cup"; *The New Renaissance:* "Root River" (under the title "Root River Poems"); *Nimrod:* "The Admiral Returns," "The Narrows," "Protector of the Indians," "A Reverse Fish"; *Outerbridge:* "Return"; *Slant:* "The Bite"; *Southern Review:* "Human"; *Tampa Review:* "Adult Love," "No Boundary"; *Terra Nova:* "Lakeviews."

"The Hunt Cup" appeared in the *Anthology of Magazine Verse and Yearbook of American Poetry, 1996,* and in *The Bread Loaf Anthology of New American Poets* (University Press of New England, 2000).

"At the Egyptian Exhibit," and "Deep Shit" appeared in *The Bread Loaf Anthology of New American Poets* (University Press of New England, 2000).

"Pigeons" was reprinted in *Urban Nature* (Milkweed Editions, 2000).

"Myth of the Flood" appeared in *Hammer and Blaze* (University of Georgia Press, 2002).

My thanks also to the following for their helpful advice on many of these poems: Ruth Anderson Barnett, Bruce Beasley, Christine Casson, Janet Holmes, Suzanne Paola, Martha Rhodes, Bill Thompson, Ellen Bryant Voigt, and Bill Wenthe. Finally, I want to thank The National Endowment for the Arts for the aid of a fellowship in poetry that gave me the time to write some of these poems.

dedicated to Christine Casson

The world is the closed door, it is the barrier.
And at the same time, it is the way through.

—Simone Weil

Contents

Double Life

ONE

Homage to Bosch

All flesh is grass, and all goodliness thereof
is the flower of the field.
—Isaiah 40:6

And it was done. The universe a clear ball
gathering dust on nothing's highest shelf,
its snows drifted to mists from which the earth
rises, *en grisaille,* to its first morning.
Rivers and valleys. Rolling hills. Mountains
quickened from the ash of their vanishing.
A landscape colorless, before memory,
pierced by a ray from the receding whirlwind.
Above, sad-faced, ringed by clouds, God opens
his *Summa,* book of judgment and of straw.

I.

Our procession filed through the opened gates
  of the Prado, leaving behind
the guitarists, sword-sellers, bronze horsemen
  of Madrid. Forty schoolboys,
faces daubed with acne, what did we know
  about the provinces of art?
We'd have preferred the hotel pool, tapestries
  of beachtowels, bikinis,
bold impastos of the Ramblas, Torremolinos.
  Through rooms of portraits, scions
of history, I shadowed like the town fool
  who stumbles into a coronation.
Then, more fabulous than a roadside carnival:
  The Garden of Earthly Delights—
swarms of nudes, drunk on the juice of berries
  bigger than balloons, tumbling
in the soft grass among seeds of pomegranates,
  enormous fish, shimmering
bubbles housing lovers, kingfishers, goldfinches
  parading toward the cavalcade
(a bestiary turning back on itself like a serpent
  eating its own tail) circling
the central pool. Was this sin or innocence,
  to skinny-dip with dragonflies,

paddle downstream in an apple-boat, or don the head
 of an owl to dance flamenco?
The thirteen-year-old I was woke to the choices:
 On the left wing, the Garden,
Christ in the gesture of a healer taking Eve's hand,
 Adam looking on, his feet
touching the divine gown while behind them the Fountain
 of Life pours out its rivers.
And on the right, the furnace-city of Hell,
 like a photograph of Dresden;
musicians crucified on harps, an enthroned demon
 with a chamber pot crown
defecating the damned into torment's cesspool.
 Only now, years later, do I see
in the background of Paradise that lion rending
 the carcass of a deer,
how it's mirrored in the monster who's turned
 into a macabre Tree of Knowledge,
the sharp limbs piercing the cracked eggshell of skin
 in which devils sit at table—
as if evil had fashioned a tavern in the guts. . . .
 That summer drifts, *sfumato,*
in the haze of memory: the Prado, Toledo,
 Ávila, Montserrat, a man
collared by soldiers on the line to Gibraltar,
 beaten senseless, dragged off.

II.

How plentiful the world is, a wagon piled to bursting
 with its golden trove of hay, wheels wobbling
 underneath, squeaking, the great load teetering
 in every rut.

We parade it through harvest fields, imagining before us
 towns untouched by plague, abuzz with a babble of markets,
 revels uninspired by the feast days of saints—
 a kingdom of our own.

For us, every day is Mardi Gras. We crowd the driven cart
 in scarlet tunics, emerald buskins, royal robes,
 pale turbans, homespun wools, muslins and silks
 as we whirl ahead in our St. Vitus Dance.

We trundle like an army through leveled forests once rife
with deer, wild boar, the ghosts of extinct species,
while behind us lands spread out in shimmering haze
as on the third day of creation.

Lords, emperors, archbishops, kings, their pockets heavy
with the weight of tithes; knights mantled in armor
speckled with the blood of crusades; ruminant clerics,
all train in back, marking their lots like destiny.

Where a jigging burgher clutches his purse to his heart,
another pitches his ladder to the wain, hoping to climb
atop to where a courtier with lute serenades a maid.

Do they hear the song below, those tearing at the stack,
tearing at each other as they're crushed
beneath the wheels?

The feasters turn away, sweet smells exuding
from the campground—a pig's head roasting on its spit,
trout on poles awaiting flame, casks of wine. . . .

Still we progress in our exodus, riotous as the rabble
who fashioned a golden calf.

And what if, human, we were blinded by such fullness,
cajoled by subaqueous demons who would brandish our heads
on pikes—who's to say our fate could be otherwise?

The saint crouches in reverence over his testament, prey
for spirits who taunt him from an altar spread
with bread and wine.

Or from the hollowed trunk of an oak the temptress calls
his name, fingering herself, while flying fish,
bird-boats, ascend infernal skies.

The sufferings of the damned and saved, how alike they are—
as if the Almighty sharpened his blade for all equally,
and the arms extended in universal blessing
were only the austere gesture of some bitter judgment.

And so that faint glow on the horizon must be Utopia,
earthly paradise, the torchlights of the millennium
and final consummation burning in the eyes of a thief
who slits his brother's throat for a fistful of straw.

III.

In Carpentras the dead are rising,
   joined by angels,
stunned to ecstasy by the beneficence
   of light that lifts them
into its tunnel, a blinding cornucopia.
   Assumed, do they forget
the desecration of their bodies?
   Or have they accomplished
in their passing what we cannot:
   forgiveness,
even of unimaginable horror?
   I cling to my wrongs—
how as a child I couldn't pull the wings
   off butterflies
at other's egging, but secretly wished
   for the deaths
of those boys who'd surround me
   after school, faces
turned into a canvas of leering masks;
   or my own betrayals—
the friends outgrown, lovers left,
   family denied.
Puffed as Midas who fingered all he saw
   into gold,
I acclaim my ambition to exceed
   and call it virtue,
the way a dandy admires his image
   in a mirror.
Is this, then, goodness: the arm of a boy
   suddenly gone limp
when, charged by hurt, he most desires
   to strike?
Is that why so often the world appears
   unbearable,
because what is most truly us—the part
   that suffers—
can't free itself from the cramped room
   we've furnished for it
in the remotest mansion of ourselves?
   In that barn,

the bewildered child accepts the gifts
    of this world,
while behind him on the torn plain
    crazed horsemen clash.
Too soon he'll wake to the nightmare
    of mocking faces
that crowd him till his own is obscured
    in the rush of torture,
the driven cross. . . . I bear on my back
    the weight of my own skin.

—

Bones on the road. A wreckage of weapons.
In clear light killers tie their victim
to a tree as another man hunkers off,
abandoned to his dream of refuge.
There are lovers in meadows, pipers
in fields. And on a far hill a throng
gathers for an execution. Through this land
the wanderer passes, his staff edging back
a rabid dog. . . . Empty One, Unnamable,
only by your command are we sustained.

TWO

Keats's Coffee Shoppe

A thing of beauty is a joy forever
I read below the rim of the paper cup
my harelipped waitress hands me,
the sky blue urn on its curve
framed by Corinthian columns.
Behind her, real urns, tall coffee drums,
release steam from heavy lids,
rumbling faintly, while rings of burners
blaze underneath like tribal fires.
Signs hawk specials to the clientele
milling in from Third: day-shift workers,
garrulous with shoptalk, packing booths;
retiree couples arrived like clockwork,
taking their time; the high school hordes
crowding counters for burgers, egg creams.
Some muse over dog-eared menus
splotched with years, held under the gaze
of thumbtacked icons, madonnas
taped above tarnished gothic fountains,
though always there's someone sitting alone
breaking bread with shaking hands.
How at home they all seem, even
the worn-out waitress, despite the heat
and perpetual racket from the kitchen,
a babble of shouting tongues,
as if behind the scene some demiurge
were in full production, serving up fates
that *will never pass into nothingness*. . . .
I, too, could linger into quiet hours,
easeful amid the grease and splendor.

The Bite

The boy on the talk show has no face,
only the mask the doctors made through a miracle
of grafts and plastic. Beside him, his mother
fingers her neck-chain cross; and when the camera
flashes the old photo we catch a glimpse
of innocence, dark-haired, smiling. Too bad
the glib host can't avoid the nervous platitude:
"You must be a very brave young man. . . ."

Of course he must, as the host quells the curious:
"Did it hurt? Were you scared?" and even then
the story's worse than the palpable horror
broadcast to our several million homes,
so odd it sounds almost a fairy tale: a bite
suffered while he played too near the woods
slowly burned away the flesh until the venom
satisfied itself with what was most his own.

What could they do in a village so backward,
so far south, in another hemisphere?
Surely here they'd find a cure for him.
Or, in another stab to ward off the fear,
Don't they still rattle fetishes there?
But the mind recoils—a bug could do that—
and remembers Actaeon who stumbled on
the naked goddess, was eaten by his own hounds.

Transmitted into our lives like a vision,
the boy clarifies our fate somewhere
between terror and survival, and turns us
away to face the spider in the woodpile—
black widow or fiddleback—the snakes' nest
among stones beyond the edge of the lawn,
wrong turn into gunfire, the recessive gene
ticking in the blood: kisses of the dark God.

Articles of Faith

I. *Ark*

Suspended in desert,
fed on hunger,
we grope toward new earth
guided by a cloud
that reminds us
we are dust.
Trust me, the little room
we carry whispers
with a voice from nowhere—
in one ear the law,
in the other our bewilderment.

II. *Missal*

Palm-heavy, my childhood
missal's freighted with the weight
of what's lost: intonations,
liturgies, murmured refrains.
From its spine ribbons dangle,
splayed rainbow that would mark
my first communion place
as my fledgling soul marked time,
and the priest in Kodachrome soutane
raised his monstrance to the mystery,
facing it alone, facing away.

III. *Reliquary*

A pig, fetal, waiting for scalpels
of children to quicken it to judgment,
curled in the attitude of a plaything
abandoned, the guts an arrangement
of colored parts to be unpuzzled
with the dead's acceptance.
How nearly attentive he seems,
immersed in his jar on the shelf,
no less than the head of a saint
whose mummified eyes stare out
from the altar of fulfillment.

IV. *Veronica's Napkin*

It must have happened slowly,
the way a print's gentled
in a darkroom. Only later,
after the beatings, shame,
death, and all those rumors,
must it have seemed miraculous:
the dead man's face risen whole
into cloth. And the woman gazing at it,
as at her own face in a mirror—
gazing at something unimaginable,
indelible, gazing past the flesh.

V. *Scapular*

Flesh parts, a curtain
where pierced hands
draw away white folds.
There, crowned, bathed in flame,
the heart's revealed: love
that would cure the world's wound.
Above, how composed the face is,
as if the man grew certain
in solitude, as if he knew
words were not enough, and he needed
this last chance to show us what he meant.

Near Forty

Not to have been the old man moaning
in the bed beside me that summer
of the panic attack I thought my heart

was joy enough having heard nightlong
his incorrigible howls, not the pain
of a worn-out body gone to thrall,

but of who he had become as his hands
groped for the attendant's ample breasts
before she tied his wrists. No, he cried, no

like a child ordered to his room—so ripe
a diminishment. *There but for the grace. . . .*
Though it's wrong to say so, wrong, too, to say

I was the man, since I walked out free
of my little anguish into the world's warmth,
and quickened by its fierce summoning.

Human

Omo Dei

Dante, spurred by divine love, saw
the letter M in the human face,
sockets of the penitent
hollowed to a script
that marked the Maker's signature,
and praised it, sky-written emblem of the just,
as he ascended paradise.

But this near-noon, at millennium's end,
after a morning of pickup ball,
the only signs I see are for
the fast-food dives
where I pull in under a golden arch
that announces to the world
BILLIONS SOLD. Do they mean what
or who? For lined up as we are
we could be a train of souls
undone by suspect appetites.

By now, I should be at ease
living *in the middest,* apart
from the sure path—the way
those ballplayers in the booth across
laugh it up after a game; or the way
that child, escaped from her father,
dances up the aisle with a joyful wail,
oblivious as a dervish, ignorant
of the looks her face begets;
and ignorant of the face
that wiseass makes behind her back,
like something out of Bosch,
while the whole booth bursts out laughing.

As she makes her way back up the rows
of plastic seats, her face appears
much older than her age, her eyes
too widely spread apart, as if clay
had been too hastily fixed, the form

miscast by some uncertain hand.
Now her father gathers her away
from the muted jibes and stares,
and those like me who turn aside
fascinated by some message
hidden among our scraps
of lunch, and carries her to play outside,

where a clownish cop, his head
shaped like a hamburger,
his eyes pools of blistered paint,
stands guard over other, stranger beings.
And she climbs up with the same rapt screech
to wave at her father through the bars.

As in a Shaded Bower

1. *At the Egyptian Exhibit*

Thou shalt have power over water, breathe air,
be surfeited with the desires of the heart. . . .
—FROM AN EGYPTIAN SARCOPHAGUS

How, you said, you used to sleep—the way
the mummy's hand flared awkwardly, twisted
just so, transposings of the quick and dead
made tractable behind glass. In his day:
tombs stocked full as bomb shelters, the soul
beaked and twittering over the body's haunts,
or casting off from rushes in the sun's boat.
What scares is how I see you, not cured, gaunt
as this shell, but a child curled in your bed,
your small hand in the shape of something gone
but for its remnant. As if someone wedded
these worlds as unalike as skin and stone.
Or as though the wind had stopped to trace
its image in the sphinx's disappearing face.

2. *Adult Love*

Coming home tonight, snow trailed us up the lawn
like tossed lingerie. We kept the candles
burning after dinner, and we're young lovers again,
shucking our clothes, half expecting parents to walk in,
shocked that their babies have grown pubic hair.
But there's no one now to tell us what's forbidden.

We wear our adult skins as camouflage to guard
the child who cries anyway: for the breast, for the gesture,
for the one word that will soften its despair;
cries that wake the enemy who rampages through the house,
wild-eyed, bayonets spearing anything that moves,
unless we turn them back. And we do—with hands, fingertips,
tongues—so our sleep may be full of peace.

Lakeviews

I.

A jigsaw of breakers,
the lake like an ocean
on which a few sails bob.

Dewdrop in space
this sea of reality
the bodhisattva said,

so like the astronaut
peering back at the blue
bubble he calls home.

I skip stones at waves,
await the petering
hops—my childhood art—

and count what comes
success, hearing overhead
these gulls screeching.

II.

On the shut-down beach
empty lifeguard stands
stare blank as scarecrows

in cornfields miles
inland. We wade ankle-deep
in tides that cut

delicate scallops here,
where three months ago we saw
the child tread out

beyond the warning buoys—
Dangerous Currents. And whatever
it was that left her parents

stunned on shore, chilled
in midsummer to the bone,
swept her under, then

two towns south where
they found her, the horizon
as now a seamless edge

across which a tanker
ploughed in slow motion,
laboring somewhere north.

III.

Twenty below. And this
cauldron where floes
have frozen fast

to slick sheets,
snow-swept, seethes
in steaming patches

of bear's breath,
the surface closing in
on itself like guilty

conscience. Who
ventures these docks of ice
will feel steady

as Jesus walking
the blown waters; cold
as Jonah swallowed

whole at sea,
closed over, his hope
broken and flown.

IV.

I follow the berm
out to the Pike's mouth,
sluggish swells

where the sandbar
forms, reforms in wakes
the wind flays, warming.

In the shallows
a fisherman tugs his line.
Stench of alewives

washed by thousands
ashore. Polished
stones at my feet.

Shards of light,
like strobes of a signal gun,
flash in the tide.

THREE

Return

My old best friend from home
confesses he hasn't read
a book for twenty years,
says he wants to know
how it is I could devote
most of my life to words.
I tell him it could happen
anywhere, in a bar
just like this one—*Skinflints,*
its name two strong stresses
that marry flesh and stone:
Good friends meet after years,
one who stayed—a wife,
three daughters, his job
as auditor landing him
a detached house at the shore;
the other returned, his life
solitary, picked up
from school to school.
"Can I buy you a beer?"
one friend asks, and soon
they're in each others'
histories, a part of them
rehearsing different lives,
until the one who came back
wakes inside himself, begins
piecing together these scraps
shared beneath the music's
hum, as though uncoding
an ancient scroll. On the walls
the pictures come alive—
Coney Island, 1904:
the boardwalk a dazzle
of people and lights;
V-J Day, 1945:
sailors standing out
from the crowd, fists raised,
their faces beaming, a world

composed in black and white.
And should someone snap
a picture, these two
distant for so long would glow
with such congruencies. . . .
But really, it's nothing
like this for my friend
and me. The new crowd
filters in while our pasts
fumble through our fingers
and unreel and silence
spreads like smoke between us.

Rooms

1. *Pearl Court*

for Kevin Tobin

Two beds. Two dressers. A mirror. A hope chest.
Cracked plaster we fresco with art conceived
in crayon, tempera—our private Lascaux.
In the window you prop a telescope
divining worlds beyond the rowhouse yards
while I fiddle in bed with my baseball cards
cursing duplicates. And once upon a time,
Father Bolger blesses our sanctum, and the ceiling
crashes down with escaping ghosts.
Remember it all, the strewn uniforms, divisions
of toy soldiers, muted arguments, that passage
through our parents' room to leave the house?
How they raise themselves around us still, those walls
accustomed to the double-life of longing.

2. *Euclid Avenue*

for M.C., M.H., and M.V.

A chill breeze off the Sound disturbs the shade
in a painted-open window of a living room
I lived in: a clutter of books and knickknacks.
In that low-rent dive we'd gather nightly,
avant garde of our blue-collar college,
to tinker with drinks and table talk.
Cum Vino Veritas. The new Lost Generation.
Phosphors basking in our own light.
There, beside us, our shadow-selves convened
their own rapt salons of coffee-break chats
and sports page banter, our fathers musing weather.
Yet we would be, as Cavafy said, citizens
of a city of ideas—though we enter the gates
in rags, dragging the slave-life behind us.

3. *Divinity Hall*

All night I dream of fires, consuming the room,
or making a crown of flame around the bed,
till I'm jolted bolt upright, then fall back.
Embers flare in the sealed-up hearth.
And something in the hiss of kindled ash
beckons me to enter, supplicant,
like the saint who longed to lose herself
in God: *In this center dwelling place*
the seeker finds repose; the intellect,
amazed, peers through its small crevice
at what surpasses sense. Promiscuous peace.
Pentecostal silence. But the heart,
that green log, stifles at what might have been:
flash point, backdraft, the soul blown free.

4. *Edenvale Road*

A spate of marbles scuttering from on high,
though it was more like paw-clicks on parquet
the way those hailstones pattered the roof
of a top-floor bed-sit in Ranelagh.
Nothing clicked, or everything. Whole days
crouched over my earnest dabblings, Harps
and chips from the Paradise Take-Away,
I'd listen for a hush at the heart of sound.
No sound. So let the masters witness:
"A man sits and carves a piece of wood
and out of it comes god." And out of this
what profit? In-breakings. Parings. A furtherance
of the work. The wish to add a single stone
to the boundless house we live in.

House Hunting

Also they have temples and sacred places in which
the gods really dwell, and they hear their voices
and receive their answers. . . .
—PLATO, *Phaedo*

Our realtor reminds me of my freshman
philosophy teacher, a would-be Cagney
with midlife spread filling out
the blue sport coat and gray pants.
As he flips through keys, small-talking,
dismissing all before finding the one
that clicks open the lock, I can almost see
Professor Azar leaning over his desk,
doing his best to sell forty blank stares
on the virtues of virtue.

Few of us cared
to get his ad hoc lectures salvaged
from dead air, Socratic jibes
fallen cold as sparks in Plato's Cave,
each of us intent on a reel of shadows
flickering like television in our heads,
while he'd have trooped us through a world
of Forms, which was what he loved best,
the soul's furnishings arranged in perfect
rooms of thought,

each attribute without flaw—
like the whitewashed walls of this parlor
hung with the owner's family portraits
grown forlorn in his absence, as though
lifted from their fixtures they floated
through space, no longer here, like us
watched by what's foreign,
as we imagine ourselves at home—
this sofa our couch, these knickknacks
shipped to somewhere else, shelves
filled with books, and each studied room
a dream of forgotten life.

Our realtor takes such care,
pointing out cracks in plaster, slippages
of kitchen tiles, floorboards, runs his eye
across walls, ceilings, checks the basement
circuit box, wanting, it seems, what's best
for us, inspecting the house as if it were
an argument of the world's soundness,
in every niche a subtlety. And we follow
like disciples who want to believe
Here is where we belong, sunlight
burnishing the windowpanes, the dust
hazed and swirling like first stars.

Miranda

From my window I watch the flurries whirl
Milan into dream, and clothe the duomo's dome
in robes of sheerest gauze. Each day the faithful
haul more marble to the masons, sculptors,
busy at their arts. Turrets, spires rise
beside brave saints, gargoyles—so elaborately slow,
like a masque whose movements bore us to belief.
My father's down below, all thoughts dead, blind
to this prospering. They say it will take centuries.
He sleeps between a bishop and a Medici.

I never knew why he named me for wonder;
or was it my mother. No matter—
in the backward of time he's nearly all I knew.
To this day, however hard I try, I remember
nothing of my life before exile, only vague shapes
of handmaids in gowns, indistinguishable
as statues in this snow, indistinguishable
as those doting on me now. I do not know
my mother's face. It's as if memory itself
were my father's shifting island, full of noises;
though however hard I listen, her spirit's voice
is one I never hear. But I hear his still,
turbulent as the storms he'd conjure at a whim,
or justify by some auspicious star.

For hours he'd linger in his cell
that was dank and claustral as a monk's hut
poring over books, talking to himself,
or summoning powers I could not see
while I spied darkly through a wall of reeds.
Intonations. Biddings. Gibberish. His lips
moved like the tremblings of a bird,
so different from when he'd speak to me.
So when he cloistered himself,
that's when I'd feel most free
pretending to have run of the island.
These were my spirits: hidden springs gushed
from the forest floor, moss-slicked stones,

swollen lagoons, the hush of palms
in quickening winds, huge fronds that drooped
sullenly and smelled of skunk, sweet pulp
of outsized fruits, tidal hiss; the poked eye
of a jellyfish in the foam, dolphin plash
in a glitter of waves. And best of all,
the tulips, dark-hearted and voluptuous,
that I'd linger over, almost tasting
their color on my tongue.

Sometimes in those times alone
I'd lie among dunes and dream an island
full of people; or muse myself a strong god
with power to sink the sea beneath the land.
To think of it after so many years, I see now
how near I was to the first child
of those shores. Was he really so very ugly?
That night, when he came to my bed, misshapen
thing, and spoke to me, and put his hand
over my mouth, I could hear my father's voice
in his consuming eloquence, and the same
mastering need to control.

Little joy after that, till the storm,
till Ferdinand, bestowed from the sea.
How could I not be drawn to him, for twelve years
having known no one but those two, no one
of my sex? I liked his body, liked his laugh,
though he wanted as lover, always troubled
by affairs of court. Still, he had a tenderness.
Awkward prince, my king, that's what I clung to
years after the vow diminished to chess games
at night in the parlor. Sometimes, I wish
we had stayed on the island, spurned the contract,
the promises of state, spurned my father's wish.
I remember how they spoke that day, past and future
aside, like conspirators, plotting my life,
as if I were nothing more than my father's gift.
Milan, the island, Naples, again Milan. . . .
I'm tired of the tricks of dukes and kings,
how always they turn to the audience for approval,

childish ploy to make them feel they're loved.
My father's dead these forty years, my husband nearly ten,
who together made me queen. Let the others fade,
all courts and counselors, gaggles of men preening
in costume. But I'll remember Caliban,
who like me lost a mother to the arts of men.
How often I think I see his shape in the shape
of this cathedral's carved stone—creature whose voice
is rain and wind, grimacing under its weight.

Two Playthings

> *Human history is simply the history of servitude*
> *which makes men—oppressor and oppressed alike—*
> *the playthings of the instruments of domination. . . .*
> —Simone Weil

1. *Pigeons*

Beaks evolved for gutter cracks, handouts.
Hooked toes fit for a witch's brew.
Indigent as bag ladies, as self-possessed,
we halt traffic at a lunatic's whim,
pecking at scraps, muttering to ourselves,
our roosts under eaves, in rooftop cages.
What face under heaven has a duller eye?
Yet who would begrudge our one consummation:
to outlast you in love, impassioned daylong
where we've homed on your sill, your flesh spent
with work or weariness? Untouchables,
we croon indiscriminately our garbled moans
till you drive us out. Our shit can eat through steel.

2. *Brief Elegy for a Subdivision*

Here lawns grow long-haired like the dead,
homes boarded up, a breeze through shattered panes
crooning hollow blues for what's left behind.
Now children race their bikes in other suburbs,
mothers calling after them, invisible hands
tugging at their dress hems. What did the Seneca
name these paved fields? If only we remembered
we could chant it like a spell to chase the wronged
spirit from its bed, the groundswell churning
under our feet; or cast it into swine that would squeal
into waters that gnaw the scrags of a continent,
and wash to the feet of its proud mansions
waves hissing foam through the sea's teeth.

Root River

Moorings

Imagine nothing here: the boats released—
yachts with names like *Harbor Belle, Wingspread,*
outboard rafts for excursions of the poor.
These slips dispersed like sands at North Beach,
scalloped runoffs in the glitter and detritus

of this fractal shore, churning its definitions.
Nothing here. As if the flimsy rigging
of who you are could catch a breeze
that blew back to beginnings, and you'd know
what you were before you were: flung spray,
slow tongue of a glacier on moraine,
ice floes, sheen on the bank, gnashed pebbles,
a slippage of tides emptied into fullness.

Factory

The clock in the tower of the old
Horlick Factory still keeps time. Its Roman
numerals harken back to days elapsed
with shunts of carriages, wooden wheels,
workers shuttling through twelve-hour shifts

in the grind and vistas of the nineteenth
century. They log their sweat, sons-of-sons,
till gearwheels revolve to blenders, bytes.
Think of Malthus, of Marx in his flat,
Darwin driven to destiny on *The Beagle,*
Vanderbilt, surfeited, extending his trusts.
Or, rather, think of this river, its currents
channeled, the flow accepting and accepted.

Quarry Dam

A line's flung across current, below falls,
its fly old bristles twisted, makeshift.
But this time, along its length, the boy's
fastened hooks, so beneath the surface
it's an illegal snag the fish swim towards.

Perched on the bank, sneakers slicked with mud,
wrist flicking a five and dime rod and reel,
he hasn't begun dreaming about fleshpots
in Thailand; of the dragon he'll have tattooed
behind his ear; or of the cell he'll keep
after knifing a man to death. A salmon
strikes. Another. The escapees float,
flanks torn open, to the muck of the shore.

Interstate

Gothic bracings, rivets dispersing stress,
exhaust burn on concrete, oil slick, skid tracks,
rust bled from railings, chipped grillwork of rods,
hair cracks, a firmament stitched with steel,
the gust of traffic blowing north, south. . . .

Below: cropped meadows, lacquered rocks at brookside,
crooked arm of dead oak diving into reeds.
The river takes what's given and moves on,
as if the slather and hiss of origin
drew presence from every hollow, each jam
and bend—a backdrop, ignored till something
quickens, like the snipe plunging through space
that disturbs the calm of the surveyor's eye.

Headwaters

Of course you couldn't follow them, car-bound,
map-weary, staking a back street trail
through town, intent on this river that runs
back on itself, banks harboring dead ends,
parks whose paths open to no *aporia*.

So strike out again, now on foot,
fathoming the blind fronts of neighborhoods,
lives marked in a moment's opacity,
into outskirts, noting the names of towns—
Mount Pleasant, Oak Creek, Hale Corners, Husher.
There, where the river dwindles to posted fields
beyond the latest subdivision, you'll find it:
indigent spring, your end, its beginning.

FOUR

No Boundary

> *And every space that a man views around his dwelling place,*
> *standing on his own roof or in his garden or a mount*
> *of twenty-five cubits in height, such space is his universe.*
> —Blake, "Milton"

Boundless though finite the universe lives
in increments of imagination,
galaxies pulsing with lust to be human,
as if the music of the spheres
chimed to Bach and breakage, and shattered glass
were prelude to a Mozart concerto. . . .

I put down the book, leave my study
with its volumes stacked like extinctions
on the shelves: bright, April day,
the sun unobscured by cloud. Barefoot,
pants rolled above my knees, I see
the garden's newly tilled, its hegemony

of vegetables, flowers, herbs
unrisen into their predestined places;
and beyond, the house with its levels of brick
and untarnished trim, its windows'
burnished clarity, ripe for a spread
in *Better Homes* or *Life:* My solid world.

But how hard to think of entropy:
planets hurled into space
that is its own yo-yo whirling them
back again; or a family on vacation,
arriving home before they left,
their deaths greeting them at the door.

The mind breaks like a child's favorite toy.
A woman collapses on her husband's coffin,
her face smiling with grief
while memory's black hole cradles him
in her arms. Still, I could dwell here,
physicist of the familiar, till the moon,

that magician's coin, slipped
behind the neighbor's house; till stars
woke in the skull's planetarium—
a first man, imperial homo-sapiens,
and that wouldn't be enough.
I could feel, lying in grass,

that there are no boundaries, my body
a sun burning on its own horizon—
though imagination's never brave enough
to open all the rooms of its mansion,
its gardens where time,
for an instant, inhabits itself:

where the least force, gravity, proves
the greatest, though longing persists,
as if "to be" and "to love" were one
conjugation. Or as if this ant that crawls
on my ankle, inspecting my birthmark,
posed no threat, thinking me the earth.

The Locksmith

On time nearly to the minute, he drives up
to my curbside in a van that reads APEX
and the message *Jesus—The Real Key* scripted
on its side; then eases over to me where I stand
near the stoop, sweaty, my hands soiled
from weeding, his big boots clopping up the walk,
the crown of his cowboy hat peaked
above his head. "Summer finally got here,"
he says, though it's nearly fall. I laugh,
nodding, make the usual small talk
before he goes about his business, deft
as a devotee and done in no time.
It's afterwards when we sit to look over
the bill that he asks, "Do you go to a church
in town?" I lie and tell him I'm Unitarian.
He tells me he does their locks too, then nods
seriously to me on the stairs. "John tells us
there's one absolute—You have to be baptized
in the spirit to be saved, it's the only way."
It amazes me how easily such talk brings me back
to days of candles, chrism, bread ghosting the tongue,
incense and retreats, though I never cared
for that pretense of a chosen people, *the wages
of sin is death,* and want to tell him
I no longer envy such certainty, that I prefer
the stony ground, the mustard seed of faith
hollowed by doubt, that it's only the observance
of words I keep now to stay the soul.
But I stay silent, let him go on with his history
of wives lost, children gone bad. "There's no peace
like the voice of God speaking inside you,
loud and clear as my own now—it's no wonder
the wealthy and well-educated rarely get saved,
heads all cluttered with ungodly things."
Then his homespun parable of how mine
is a marginal neighborhood, that my house
is a house at risk: "Hell is living for eternity
with those people two blocks over." I think

I should tell him to leave now, certain myself
of where I stand, but I am the one who called him
to change the locks, and let him stay—
my old grudging failure to confront.
As he goes I thank him, and he thanks me
for listening. When his van turns the corner
up the street, I turn back to my dubious lawn
miles from the county where he lives,
wind blowing through the long prairie grass,
his sweet fields whispering *Jesus, Jesus.*

Myth of the Flood

After the voice had made known its intentions,
and the man stood dumb behind the house
he would soon dismantle, board by board
at his wife's dismay, at the neighbor's jeering,
to fashion from its wreckage the saving boat;
after the boat had been filled to bursting
with everything needed to start life anew,
the menagerie's stench fuming in his nostrils,
choking him, a cacophony in his ears
as though he were housing Chaos itself;
after the first slow drops, then the downpour
that made it seem the heavens were oceans,
the jeers turned to pleas, and the pleas in vain;
after The Great Absence, the slow return—
a sudden hush in the bestiary's din, the man
with an olive branch between his fingers,
the waters receding to tranquil streams,
runoffs where the judged lay piled like seaweed,
their bloated bodies steaming on the slopes
and out across the plain; after all that,
as his wife freed the remnant, he made ready
the offering, slaughtered two beasts
who would not make it to the world to come;
then knelt before the pyre while the Power
that changed everything savored the burning flesh.
On the horizon: a warrior's bow thrown down
and shining, a pair of doves arrowing away.
The Power sniffed. The man had his choice of gods.

Days of Creation

With nothing in the wind's way,
who knows it's there?

—

Malignant night. A light streak
carves away absence.

—

Just blink a million years
and the sky's lowing at its reflection.

—

No fee. No cars. No crowds.
The park open through the next millennium.

—

At the master's yowza the orchestra starts;
galactic dancers whirl through the ballroom.

—

A geometric pause between sea and sky:
suddenly what could swim can fly.

—

Who knows who I am, word half-uttered,
buffeted by my own breath?

—

Dreaming Yourself into day,
You could sleep forever.

Five Exegetical Poems: A Palimpsest

1. *The Lie*

(Psalm 12)

Amicable smile, accommodating voice
insinuating from the soul's night:
"Good man, have you any choice
but to presume your labors true and right

for those you love, for those who keep unknown
in the outer dark of the world's charade."
Because children starve, and the needy groan. . . .
Yet those who come to anybody's aid

come only for a time, or for themselves.
The anchor hawks his omens on the tube—
"The President threatens force." "A mother sells
her baby to a cult." The spirit broods

while nothing stirs inside or out. Hope tells
us in the end that all comes even,
though shrewder tongues resound like bells
to rouse the demons, and the demons win.

2. *The Rift*

(Psalm 14)

The fallen preacher weeps away his sins,
and as when some latent scent wakens instinct

ten thousand dupes phone in their pledge,
keeping the shameless thief in business.

Still, how easy it is for intellect
to have its sway, commanding to dissect

more than make whole. In truth, all's askew—
wish and wisdom. And the soul asking rescue

remains untried, or turns on itself.
The devices of the spirit move by stealth,

the preachers say to succor a saving remnant.
The true heart's nourished on abandonment.

3. *The Judge*

(Psalm 82)

It's the breaking loose
of things, a shattered firmament
from which the stars rain down like glitter
on the soul's tribes, who pull down their tents,
disperse into wilderness

where no manna falls.
Wasted inner sky. On its horizon,
no ark leads the chosen, no pillar of fire,
but a figure blindfolded, cast in sun,
stands stone-still, weighing idols.

What judgment does it hold,
that teetering scale, for you? What myths
of yourself must you behold, finally, without fear?
What stunning, unspeakable realms
open behind the blindfold?

4. *The Heart*

(Psalm 73)

Though all temples topple
and wind remakes the stone,
we would call each other home
so that what is empty fills

with something more than time.
All hearts are Babylon,
self-conquering, self-blind,
till each gives up its throne

and deems another chosen.
What would be blamed is blessed.
And we would choose this now

to bewilder the unknown
in the temple of our flesh,
in the temple of our vow.

5. *The Ways*

(PSALM 1)

Now voices sleep and soul lies down alone,
its whims like chaff taken by the air.
In the end of our ends all ways are one.

What's life like from the loftiest station
beyond the human, to which the dust aspires,
though voices sleep and soul lies down alone?

Empty dreams. Empty figures. A ship carved in bone
charts its hero on a passage to where,
in the end of our ends, all ways are one.

All things sentient endure in delusion,
the sages say, and that's the world's despair,
till voices sleep and soul lies down alone.

But who except the few—witness Origen—
would exclude the damned from vengeful fire?
In the end of our ends all ways are one

with the quest that beckons inside the question
of what we'll see when the mirror shatters,
and voices sleep, and soul lies down alone.
In the end of our ends all ways are one.

The Visit

This is how the monsignor entered
our class: without a knock, a figure
in black (but for the white collar, hair,
the blossomed cheeks) filling the doorframe,
then striding before us in a haze
of chalk dust. Attention! Sister Millietia's
lifted arms signaled as we bolted
to our feet, forty chosen children
who'd been warned to keep watch.

Above the blackboard, cardstock
Easter scenes adorned the walls
like subway advertisements.
There, Christ rode to Jerusalem,
crowds praising, waving palms;
transfigured bread while apostles
gazed awestruck; endured stations,
was crucified—though in the center
of it all he rose, arms outstretched,
above a purple-lettered HOSANNA.
"Be seated," the deep voice intoned,
and we collapsed into our chairs.
"Who can recite the great commandment?"
Twenty hands fired into the air.

Outside, clouds gathered over rowhouses,
apartments, maple-lined streets;
over St. Anselm's Church
across the alley, its swirls
of copper marble and stained glass
rising from a border of hedges.
Where swallows dive-bombed for shelter
in its steeple, the sky billowed
black, green, deep violet—a vast bruise
over the neighborhood. The drone
of the visit fell away: I was adrift
on an ocean whose waves crashed
over the boat where I lay on my back,
staring at an inscrutable thunderhead.

A lightning bolt cracked down.
And I saw in the whirlwind an angel
take shape, fierce, faceless,
aiming to plunge its pike into my heart—

then *crack* again as the nun's palm
struck my cheek, "Stop daydreaming."
The priest resumed his important lesson.
I could hear the heavy drops
begin to fall, hailstones rapping
madly against glass, each burning
its heart away like an indelible seal
into the cracked, effaced mortar of the sill.

The Hunt-Cup

It's a long time since the dawn chase over shires,
hoofbeats gathering in the half-light, human wails,
and the dog-pack barking in earnest, surging
for the flash through gorse, the prey manic for its lair,

leaping over tree roots, rifling through thickets,
desperate as the fugitive whose fear encodes the wind.
Now the escaped slave can rest on his long journey north,
the scars of chains, whippings healed to infant's skin;

now the last Jew left in the ghetto, a pack
of stormtroopers trained on his shivering body,
can stand in the open singing his lost ones home;
and the children of Kurdistan, El Mozote,

of Armenia, Capetown, Kigali, Sarajevo,
of all the cities of unremembered death,
have rewound the black scrolls of their intestines
and are dancing in the squares in a joy before language.

It's an Indian summer evening in New Hope.
And our host has served us sherry in a hunt-cup,
its sterling stem a fox's head sniffing the air
like Anubis reared in judgment over the dead

who would drink of the waters of forgetfulness:
a sweet bouquet and perfect finish. Nowhere do men
bend over their riven trophy, draining its life,
partaking of this chalice as if it housed a god;

nowhere has the wind stopped dead in its tracks,
like a mother in the aftermath of massacre
refusing the offered cup, the whole world
distilled into a thimbleful of blood.

Deep Shit

I can't remember the name of the gaunt monk
who stroked my face during confession
years ago in that bare abbey room,
Tell me what's wrong, son, tell me what's wrong,
his fingers soft as a grandmother's, his eyes
deep and pleading; nor can I remember
what I told him—something about the pain
of feeling alone, something grim and adolescent—
my back arched against the wall. *Deep shit,*
I said to myself, *You're in deep shit,*
though his hand didn't travel any further,
and I confessed my sins, forgave the indiscretion.
Afterwards, I walked out along a road
puddled by afternoon rain as I whispered the prayer
of the lost—something facile and earnest,
something parroted and true: *Show me the way.*
Before I knew (Who could make this up?),
I was ankle-deep in cow dung, deep shit,
my life already steeped in allegory:
Christian hunkered in the Slough of Despond,
Everyman forsaken by all but Good Deeds.
Though now it's *Midnight Cowboy* I think of,
how Joe Buck discovers he'll do anything
to keep alive—turn tricks in dank theaters,
bash an old man's face with a phone to save
Ratso his friend, who dies anyway.
I'm lonely, lonely the crazed Queen howls,
root of all evil, before he presses our hero
to kneel and Joe, pure of heart, breaks free
into the sleazy New York night, his journey
to the promised land of Florida begun
in the waste he's made of his life, his deep shit:
Deep shit, or whatever it is, even mishandled,
that draws us somehow beyond ourselves—
what moved the old priest to stroke my face,
his need to touch, to be touched, more powerful
than any vow. Yes, it's lonely, lonely,

like the nameless crosses of the abbey graves
where the monks perform their final wordless prayer,
O deep shit to be sure—something broken
and unbearable, something ineluctable and long.

FIVE

Homage to Bartolomé de Las Casas

In this century, and moment, of mania
Tell me a story.

Make it a story of great distances. . . .
—Robert Penn Warren, "Audubon: A Vision"

Proem: The Narrows

For here between two worlds, another, harsh,
This third, of water, tests the word. . . .
—Hart Crane

From our roof in Brooklyn I could see the Narrows
through an alley between rowhouses, and ships
churning beyond Shore Road into Gravesend
and, further, beyond Sandy Hook into the Atlantic.

Even at night, in fog, the lights of the Verrazano,
like a necklace hung on nothing, shimmered.
Freighters, tankers, sounded through absence
and, sometimes, Visitation's bells would ring in answer.

Home was the only story told to me. I'd climb
over the seawall at low tide to squat on rocks
slick with moss, and palm the water. And the river
touched me back, though I knew only one of its names.

I. The Admiral Returns

In 1493, at the age of 18, Bartolomé de Las Casas, son of a Spanish businessman, witnessed Columbus's triumphant return from the new world when "The Admiral of the Ocean Seas" paraded through the streets of Seville with seven Taino Indians, exotic parrots, and other spoils of his journey. . . .

In that time so new and like no other
the sum of what we are exceeds the known.
On hill and river the Spanish sun burns,
while throughout the town bells speak in tongues
and crowds swarm before the Arch of Images
to capture a glimpse of the miracle

parading through the square. "It's a miracle
they've come back at all," someone says. Others,
concentrating on the arch, its images
of glories past, begin to stir with the unknown.
Beggar, soldier, tradesman, don—rumors burn
along the air until, at once, all tongues

cry out to greet the pageant, as if the tongues
of angels rose exultant at some miracle:
"*Christum ferens,*" "new settler," his name burned
flagrant in the book of fame. Mothers
lift children to witness things to make the known
pale, shudder before the rush of images:

seven natives, sporting feathers, each the image
of a wild bird, and birds behind, their tongues
clacking each to each like those natives who know
no one, huddling to themselves, chained miracles
painted bright as stained glass, alike as brothers
beneath flapping banners as curiosity burns

like temptation in the soul's continent, burns
like an inquisitor's pyre—as if the scrimmage
with "Hell" were won, Jews banished, the other
infidels routed, heretics plied with tongs
to mark the one true path in this miracle
year given to God and conquest. He will own

the like of these, the young man in the crowd, known
for his family, his good breeding. As on an urn
the animal's brought to sacrifice, a miracle
of nature, though not created in the image
of God, so these seven born of a different tongue—
barbarians—march where no one asks another

"Is this all that can be known of miracles,
a god's twisted image cast in gold, the tongue
ripped burning from the mouth of the other?"

II. New World

In 1502, Bartolomé himself sailed for the Indies and lived for many years like the other colonists, holding slaves on his encomienda, or plantation, in Hispaniola (called Arimao) steadily improving his lot with the colonial governors despite taking vows as a chaplain. . . .

Scent of sweet gum rising
from night fires, dawn
lacing the palms, cedars
wide as oxen, the moon
a pale shield dissolving
in the west. This morning,
awash in mist, the *cay*
could be a caravel
and the young man who wakes
to his chosen vistas
the watchman who spotted
the providential flock.
Below his villa, *bohios*
stir with families,
gentle sheep entrusted
by God to our care,
now assembled, now marched
inland along paths
glutted with cassava,
canopied with grapes.
To him the future's
a navigable sea,
branch plucked from the tides,
covered with dog roses—
a prophecy, a sign.
Out of sight: the rivers,
children hunching for gold;
out of sight: the mines,
baskets of hands
buzzing with flies. . . .

III. A Baptism

It was not until 1514, sometime after witnessing the massacre at Caonao, Cuba, during the Pacification that Fray Bartolomé eschewed "the savage writ" of the encomienda system. . . .

Always when we entered a province
it was the same, the people plentiful
as the wild grapes above our heads,
a hundred loads within the circle
of a crossbow's shot;
                                        and me, banding
the children together to be baptized
while the soldiers pursued their customs,
not content with what was freely given,
but raiding stores, raping wives and daughters.
The natives honored me for the comforts
I'd give,
            till I became in their eyes
like their own magicians, priests, healers,
and they'd do reverence, knowing I meant no harm.
That morning, outside Caonao, our troop
breakfasted in a riverbed, only a few
small pools where the sky reflected
like torn pieces of a robe. It was full
of whetstones, and the men desired

to sharpen their swords on them.
Thousands greeted us in the town square,
some bringing gifts—cassava bread and fish,
gourds filled with water—others squatting
as is their custom, staring, frightened
at our mares. One of the mounted soldiers
drew his sword, and in a heartbeat
a hundred followed.
                                    Then, O precious Christ,
they began to rip the bellies of those lambs.
Within two credos no one remained alive,
no one in the square. Not satisfied,
soldiers flooded the groves, the *bohios,*
as I ran everywhere to stop the killing,
cursing the insolent captain's boast—
"How does Your Honor like what we have done?"

Of all those dead, one haunts me still,
that young man no older than our Lord
who wept as he bled his guts into my hands.
"If I baptize you, you will go to live with God,"
I told him, and through his anguish he said yes.
To his blood and the rest, in Christ's, I give witness.

IV. Interlude: A Reverse Fish

(Remora eel, Cuba, 1514)

Threaded through tail-fin
as through a needle's eye,
the line pays out fathoms,
trailing the mouth
through shallows to its haunt
inside the turtle's shell,
the gaping O a hook
sucking sustenance
from its bulk till both
are drawn back, instinct
plotted to technology,
the man's hand prying
the shell free of its meat,
the used tool broken
to pieces in the sand.

V. First Conversion

(Espiritu Santo, Hispaniola - Pentecost, 1514)

. . . through which so many natives lost their lives, gave up his wealth, and began to preach against the system. Called a heretic for refusing to grant penance to those holding slaves; called also a lunatic and a traitor . . . .

That morning when he pushed away from shore
in the small canoe paddled by natives,
did a light leap up from the calm of the river

calling his name? So he fell backwards
into a reverie of broken promises
and verses from Ecclesiastes—

Like the man who murders his brother
is the thief who offers sacrifice
from the possessions of the poor.

Or was it a sudden sting of fear, the sight
of his own death cruising through the brush,
whispered in the murmur of leaves, till one night

it strikes, reducing the spirit to ash?
Or maybe it was the allegory
his life was becoming, increase of a wish

that forced itself to this crux, this now
that ghosted him since home. Far-flung, fortyish,
he steadies himself in the boat's hollow,

dabbles his hand in the current, a rush
of arrows moving through reflected sky,
each scrap of shore piloted in the hush.

He might be the young man who questioned Christ
—*How can I be saved?*—and the savior
told him what he already knew, what this priest

knew the thousand times he'd read the words,
Give up everything you have, their light
finally clarified in his casting off.

Downstream, the congregation gathers
for the pliant sermon, the savage writ
sanctioned to which he'll put the sword.

Already angry faces in the flux
cry out their condemnations—*madman, heretic*—
as the quick oars lift and pierce the river's flesh.

VI. Utopias

(VENEZUELA, 1521)

. . . for fifty years Las Casas fought for native rights, traveling throughout the Indies and South America, attempting unsuccessfully to establish utopian communities where natives would share in the profits of their labors . . . .

All things are possible
in Christ, even this: to build
the New Jerusalem here, where rainforest
shields from sight the bones of tortured slaves,
abundant harvest

of the predestined,
the remnant swarming to the father's blessing
who would arrive like an unexpected god
with big plans, best intentions, the masters
trembling at his word.

Cumanna, Tuzutlan—
each name to be christened,
each city planned in the image of the One
around which the turning world revolves,
till nothing's random,

the years plotted over
to just apportions of work and prayer,
and brute and victim live together in true peace.
This is nowhere, the good man's
wish laid waste

by what? by pride?
by the system? by the judgment of his God?
Let his soul be a boat stranded in dead calm,
the captain incompetent, his hands to heaven,
waiting for wind.

VII. Protector of the Indians

(Arrival in Chiapas, 1544)

. . . advocating the Indian case in court and in his writings, serving for a time as bishop of Chiapas in southern Mexico . . . .

Those lulls were the spirit's stagnant seas
we left behind with our lost,
nine priests shipwrecked, my library
scattered to mucky shoals; behind us,
half the Spanish court praying
for my death.

So that morning
when we finally came ashore,
seeing my own people's turned backs,
hearing their curses, their obscene songs,
I steeled myself with *canciones*
sung to men bloodied as newborns,
draped in the flayed skins of their gods.
How ardently they listened, like children
spellbound by fables whose good news
would waken them from sleep.

We told them of our first parents,
their fall, of a Father's love
great enough to sacrifice his only Son
so everyone might be saved,
if only they believed. And they did:
friars baptizing them in jungle streams,
some taking vows, proof
the soul knows its true home
no matter the distances of flesh.

Even their rites, savage, the chosen
splayed alive on altars:
all raw promises of our hope.
As though truth lay buried like a seed
in earth, our coming to these lands
a gracious rain to quicken the Lord's
improbable fruit.

But these unregenerate
of my own barbarous race
who turn their backs on their God
and fashion idols of gold,
making property of their fellowmen
whom they crush like dung in the streets,
who can fathom so rank a refusal?

In my sermons I tell them this,
and pray for their redemption:
Each moment, had we eyes to see,
Christ stands before us, his body
a veil parted open, beckoning;
holding in his hand a beacon—
His own living heart torn free.

VIII. Sepulveda

(VALLODOLID, 1550)

. . . and in 1555 debating the humanist Juan Gines de Sepulveda who held that natives were "slaves by nature" and therefore justifiably subdued. Because of Las Casas's defense, the Church refused to grant its imprimatur to Sepulveda's work, and new more temperate laws were established to govern Spanish colonies. . . .

Who can deny gunpowder against pagans
is the burning of incense to Our Lord?
That morning, spoiled for the Great Debate,
I was the sword's edge of reason
to steel any cardinal's bleeding heart
against his womanlier sentiments,
upholding the perfect logic of the faith—
Christ triumphant, Christ over all.

Daylong I dispensed my syllogisms
like fine pearls before the gallery,
sensing whispered assents in the hush,
and sealed my case with Aristotle:
As the body to the soul, beasts to men,
so by nature are slaves to their masters.
What more could I have done to prove us just
save flaunting a brute bloodied with sacrifice?

Later, when the old priest entered the hall
to offer his refutation, his face
had the unshakable look of a prophet
slightly mad. Five days he droned out stories
of brutes brutalized, of brutes our equal
in the image of God—as though apes
commanded reason—and us a river
of molten flame savaging those lands.

Who'd have thought the judges could be swayed
to tolerate such folly, though I'm certain
his tact was to wear them down. You
who will witness us from a later time

note this: Las Casas was a hypocrite,
loving the distant image of himself
in native eyes till they called him father.
But I will have history's imprimatur.

IX. Second Conversion

(San Gregorio Monastery, Vallodolid, 1555)

Bartolomé de Las Casas, popularly called "Protector of the Indians," died in 1566 in Atocha Monastery in Madrid, after having written the first bill of human rights in the new world. . . .

So this is the voice
of God, the heartless
charge casting
you down
like a pearl diver
into deep, that sound
you swim through
naked, your eyes
marking fathoms
for sharks,
for the slick
treasure you pray
is there, years
of this, your hands
uncoding the bottom,
the little net you carry
permeable
as hope, your hair
grown ashen as
a prophet's,
your skin a seal's,
till one day you
emerge and
there it is: the jeweled
irritant, the perfect
pearl—

We must give back
everything.

X. Last Rites

(ATOCHA MONASTERY, MADRID, 1566)

He maintained at the end of his life that for their cruelties the colonists should be banished from their settlements so that the remaining natives may restore themselves "to their human and temporal good way of life."

A boy's perched in a tree, his hair
plaited with straw, in his free hand
a parrot he taps lightly once
on his florid crest, and it cries out
like someone driven by the sword.
Now countless parrots come, hearing
the captive, and the boy reaches
with his slender stick, a thin cord
at the end looping the birds' necks,
which he wrings, dropping them below.

The dream ends, drifts to the next
without regard, without passion
that would transform the boy into God
luring us painfully to Himself;
into history, its feathered meat
piled in millions under the tree.
Hoods hover in the claustral cell
above the wracked face of Las Casas,
the chrism a glistening film
like palm oil on his forehead,

his fingers ink-stained with tomes
written *for God alone and from*
compassion at seeing perish
such multitudes of rational men.
Fifty years—even in canoes
a cloister of books borne in crates
to Chiapas, to Verapaz. . . .
Now the hand holds out its candle,
I have done so little, a speck
of sun harboring in the dark.